Helen King

Hope of Vision Publishing
Bridgeport, Connecticut

YOU ARE NOT ALONE
Copyright © 2009 by Helen King

All rights reserved. No part of this book may be reproduced, copied, stored or transmitted in any form or by any means – graphic, electronic, or mechanical, including photocopying, recording, or information storage and retrieval systems without the prior written permission of Helen King or Hope of Vision Publishing except where permitted by law.

All scripture references are taken from The Holy Bible, New King James Version Copyright @ 1982 by Thomas Nelson, Inc.

The Maxwell Leadership Bible Copyright @ 2002 by Maxwell Motivation, Inc.

Merriam-Webster Dictionary Online Dictionary copyright © 2009 by Merriam-Webster Dictionary, Incorporated

Hope of Vision Publishing a division of HOV, LLC.
www.Hopeofvisionpublishing.com
hopeofvision@gmail.com

Cover Design: Kaye Coleman
Helen king Photo Credit: Roy Gibbons Photography
Jeffrey Paul King II Photo Credit: Kiddie Kandids

Editor: S.O.U.L.E Destiny, LLC

T.R.U.S.T
www.trustyouarenotalone.com

For more information about special discounts for bulk purchases, please contact Hope of Vision Publishing.

ISBN 978-0-9753795-5-4
Library of Congress Number: 2009940948
Printed in the United States of America

DEDICATION

To all the women all across the country and around the world who desire to have children.

He grants the barren woman a home, like a joyful mother of children. Praise the LORD! Psalms 113:9 NKJV

FROM THE EDITOR

You Are Not Alone is a compelling story of a resilient woman and her desire to birth a child. Having a personal life cradled in the biblical stories of such women as Elizabeth, Ruth, and Hannah, Helen King brings the biblical text to this current time. As the women in the Bible refused to doubt, she too was faithful and diligent until the coming of her promise.

This epic story will bring tears to your eyes and induce joy into your heart as you realize, like Helen, You Are Not Alone.

TABLE OF CONTENTS

Acknowledgement 9
My Personal Testimony 13
Prayer 19
Foreword 21
Introduction 25

PART I
Pursuit 27
How Are You Coping? 28
Did I Dream That? 30
Another Month? 31
Does He Have A Clue? 33
Learning to T.R.U.S.T. 34
Is Something Really Wrong with Me 35
Tick Tock 36

PART II
Be Still and Know 41
Renewing of Your Mind 43
Drought 45
Clutter 51
Transition 53
Core 56

PART III
Never Would Have Made It 65
Just A Prayer Away 65
Are You Ready for Your Breakthrough 67
Temptation 69

Epilogue 75
Testimonials 79
About the Author 83

ACKNOWLEDGEMENTS

To Ceabon and Nellie Jackson, you have always supported me. I have fond childhood memories because of the love you displayed. Daddy, you taught us 'A family that prays together stays together'. You made us all get on our knees in the living room and pray as a family every Friday night. Mama you bought my first bible and encouraged me to seek what God's word had to say about it. It was never too early or late to call you both. If you felt I needed you, I knew I could count on you in whatever capacity I needed. Mom and Dad, you have been the wind beneath my wings. You encourage me to fly and soar to new heights and for that I am grateful. My siblings, Sonya, CJ, Allen, Junior, Patricia and Margaret you have always made me feel protected as the baby of the Jackson family. Your encouragement, advice, and steadfastness are priceless. You have given me close to 40 nieces and nephews.

To the love of my life, Jeff, you have truly been an inspiration to me. I could not ask for a better husband. You have prayed with me and given me the push I needed when I wanted to be stagnant. You were right there when God gave me T. R. U. S. T., supporting me to write this book and to pick me up when others didn't know I was down. You had faith for us both that God would indeed bless us with children. I appreciate all you have done. God used our bumpy roads to make us stronger, wiser, and closer to each other. Our testimony has blessed others to stick it out and depend on God to be the glue in their marriage.

To my prince Jeffrey Paul King II each time I look at you I am reminded of grace and mercy because you are indeed a miracle. God has a great plan for your life. I praise him for giving you to us. To my prayer partner, Vicki, thank you for your tenacity and making it plain to me. You are truly a sister to me. You are always there to give me spiritual vision when I felt defeated. Dwayne, Jordan, and Jalyn thank you for sharing your precious jewel. Aunt Clara, I knew you would jump on board when you heard about my vision. I am appreciative of you believing in me and standing up for me when I couldn't stand up for myself. You have been right there at many pivotal moments in life. Thank you for helping me to write the vision and mission for T. R. U. S. T. (Totally Relinquishing Unto Our Savior Today and Tomorrow) in a short period of time. I am forever grateful for your support and countless amount of time you have invested in supporting the vision that God has given me. Kim White, thank you for being faithful to the ministry God has given me. You have juggled family along with other responsibilities while continuing TRUST meetings to share and encourage others. Gina Ford, you came on board and have shared with me the value of praying at anytime regardless of where I am. Thank you for looking up scriptures for me and praying for me as I wrote. To my sister-in-law Lynette, thank you for adding me to the prayer list at your church and diligently praying for me to conceive. Edwina Oliver, you told me years ago that by the time my book was to be published, I would have a picture of baby King on the cover. Guess what, you were right. However, neither of us knew that I would have more than one child. To GOD be the glory! Teressa Wade, thank you volunteering to proofread for me. I cannot express how much it meant to me for you to give countless hours of your time. To Pastor Vernon Shazier, I appreciate you mentoring me. Your advice has been valuable and carried me through many hurdles. God used you to equip me with the tools I needed to bring this book to fruition. Dr. C.E. Glover, Beulah Glover and my Mt. Bethel church family your spiritual guidance and prayers are priceless. Nova Southeastern I even thank you because the door God allowed you to close forced me to go through the door to my destiny.

MY PERSONAL TESTIMONY

God birthed the Ministry T. R. U. S. T., which stands for Totally Relinquishing Unto Our Savior Today and tomorrow into my spirit in 2001. I was listening to Donnie McClurkin's "I'll Trust You Lord." God spoke to me and told me that He wanted to use me to minister to hurting women dealing with infertility issues. There are so many of us hurting silently. There are so many of us crying silent tears. I thought that I was not worthy to carry out such a task. I went to my pastor and tried to pass it off to the church, but God would not release me. God continued to put women in my path who were hurting and going through infertility issues. The Holy Spirit sent Mr. Norman to me when I was working in an elementary school in Miramar to say, "God told me to tell you it's time." I smiled because I knew exactly what he was talking about. Then fear set in. I thought, who will I reach out to and how will I approach women on such a sensitive subject? However, 2 Timothy 1:7 reads For God has not given us a spirit of fear, but of power and of love and of a sound mind.

I got married on December 21, 1996. I thought I was using the rhythm method which is the act of abstaining from sexual intercourse on the days of my menstrual cycle (around ovulation) when I could become pregnant in order to prevent getting pregnant. In April 1997 I was diagnosed with fibroid tumors. I felt this was so unfair to my husband that I would find this out after being married only a few months. The doctor told me that I should try to conceive right away before the tumors grew. WE DID! It was fun at first but then our intimacy became a chore. In March of 1998, the tumors began to give me problems. I was scheduled to have an emergency surgery, but the Holy Spirit would not let me consent. I later found out that the surgery was for a hysterectomy. Most doctors prefer the hysterectomy where my uterus would be removed verses the myomectomy where only my tumors would be removed. Overall, the myomectomy leaves the option of having all pertinent reproductive parts necessary to conceive. I thank GOD for His grace, mercy, and divine intervention for not allowing me to have peace with the surgery.

September 1999 my menstrual cycles were so heavy and the pain was almost unbearable. I sought God out of my unbearable pain when I was in my classroom and my knees buckled from beneath me. I prayed then and there asking God for help. I went to three different doctors before consenting to surgery on May 8, 2000. I had a successful surgery, thanks to God's grace and mercy. I was so excited to get my menstrual cycle in July of 2000, because it signified I was still able to conceive. My doctor told me to give it a year to heal. Then a year and a half later in November 2001 my doctor became more aggressive because we still were unsuccessful conceiving.

Throughout the process:

    A.   I had two hysterosalpingrograms (dye is shot through fallopian tubes to check for blockage).
    B.   Prescription for Provera to regulate cycle.
    C.   Six months of Clomid (medicine to help eggs mature)
    D.   Basal Body Temperature
    E.   Ovulation Kits
    F.   Medication to shrink tumors
    G.   Laparoscopy
    H.   Two cycles with (IUI) Intrauterine insemination

Unfortunately, none of the techniques, methods, and medication was enough for me to conceive. It appeared that everyone around me was having babies, which was frustrating because I was doing everything my doctor told me to do. In June 2002 I found out that I had a small fibroid in my uterus and my right tube was clear, but the left (SVA) was blocked. I almost began to have a pity party, but my prayer partner, Vicki, helped me snap right out of it. She encouraged me and reminded me that it could be worse. That night, I was surfing the Internet and I read the story of a lady who was born with only one ovary and one tube. She wanted to know what her chances were of conceiving. I began to thank God for my complete body. After five years of trying to conceive October 2002 proved to be a milestone within my marriage and conception process. It was in October when Jeff got the semen analysis done and it took five doctor requests.

November 2004 we were told that our only option with (IVF) In Vitro Fertilization. However, God had another plan. We conceived naturally January 2005. My primary care physician told us it was a miracle when the pregnancy was confirmed. February's doctor visit we were informed that because of my medical history I would be considered a high-risk pregnancy. March's doctor visit I was diagnosed with Placenta Previa and warned of possible bed rest. May's doctor visit I was released from the specialist because the doctor's could not find anything medically wrong with the fetus. Also there were no more signs of Placenta Previa. To GOD is the Glory! Despite all of the statistical odds I was able to return to work the first seven weeks of school before going on Maternity Leave. We were tremendously blessed with a standing room only baby shower on August 20, 2005. We were in awe of all the love that was showered upon us to physically prepare us for parenthood. September 21, 2005 at 7:37AM God blessed us with a healthy baby boy. Jeffrey Paul King II was 7 lbs 9 oz and 19. 5 inches. We thank GOD daily for the miracle that he has given us. We dedicated Jeffrey back to God January 22, 2006. My journey continues as Jeff and I desire a second child. December 2007 I was told that I had a cyst and it was advised that I have a pelvic ultrasound done to monitor its size. April's visit for the third pelvic ultrasound and endometrium biopsy left me feeling defeated briefly when I was told that my right tube was enlarged. I asked what this meant and was told it usually means infection. As I lay there on the table the technician wanted to know what treatment was I on, and was surprised when I told her none. It was apparent that whatever she saw on the screen did not reflect what I was feeling. I began to praise GOD because he was letting me know that he still is in control and was taking care of me. I left that doctor's office wondering what my chances would be of conceiving a second child with the new findings that the pelvic ultrasound revealed. Then I just began to praise him for Jeffrey and I told God if you never do it again you have already given me a miracle! I thanked him for Jeffrey, our miracle baby all over again. I was scheduled for the fourth pelvic ultrasound in June of 2008 to continue to monitor the cyst even though it has broken up and appeared to be dissolving.

OUR PRAYER

A prayer of Faith for the Woman who desires to Bear Children

O Sovereign Lord, there is none like you in all the earth; from everlasting to everlasting you are God. I humbly come before your throne of grace, giving you the praise and honor that belongs to you, *From the rising of the sun to the place where it sets, the name of the LORD is to be praised. The LORD is exalted over all the nations, his glory above the heavens.* (Psalm 113:3, 4 NIV)

O heavenly Father, you have promised that if I *delight myself in you; you will give me the desires of my heart* (Psalm 37:4 NIV). Lord, as you have also promised to *"bestow favor and honor; and to withhold no good thing from those whose walk is blameless."* (Psalm 84:11b NIV). I come to you by faith, trusting in you with my whole heart to give me the desires of my heart.

O Lord Almighty, if you will only look upon your servant's heart and remember me, and not forget your servant but give me a son I promise Lord, 'To train this child up' in your word. You reward those who earnestly seek you. CHILDREN ARE A REWARD FROM YOU, I praise you for making this childless woman to keep house and be a joyful mother of children.

O Righteous Father, *Because your love is better than life, my lips glorify you. I will praise you as long as I live, and in your name I will lift up my hands.* (Psalm 63:3, 4 NIV) Thank you Lord for your divine favor.

In Jesus name, Amen

This prayer was uttered by the Holy Spirit to Sister Catherine Darville for this purpose.

FOREWORD

Helen King has written a powerful and provocative book chronicling her struggles through a long period of barrenness and her subsequent conception of what she calls her "Miracle Child." She comes from a long line of women who have dealt with the desire to have a child; only to be disappointed over and over again. The bible also chronicles women such as Sarah, Hannah, and Elizabeth who also overcame the pain of childlessness.

In biblical times a barren woman was scorned and ridiculed because barrenness was seen as a sign of God's disfavor; while fertility was a sign of the favor of God upon one's life. Hannah, for example, had a husband who loved her and showered her with gifts, neither his love nor his gifts could make up for the need she had to bear children. Hannah's emotions are evident in 1Samuel 1:10 NKJV says, "And she was in bitterness of soul, and prayed to the Lord in anguish." It was the anguish of Hannah's heart that catapulted her to the sanctuary of God. Though she lived with her agony for without change, her help came once she sought God. Her request for a son was heard by God and He answered her request and she bore a son, Samuel, who grew up to become a prophet and judged Israel.

Even though barrenness is not looked upon with scorn and ridicule today; there is still a feeling of inadequacy a woman encounters who wants to conceive and cannot.

Having personally experienced a time of barrenness in my own life, I can certainly identify with Helen's desire to have a child. I cannot count the times I cried and agonized over not being able to have a child. I had to learn to trust God and prevail in prayer for eleven years before my husband and I were blessed with our first child.

I first learned of Helen's desire for a child during one of our annual Women's Prayer Breakfasts. We were sharing what we needed God to do for us, and she shared her hurts with us. I began to pray and agree with Helen and several other sisters who were desirous of bearing children. Helen was the last of the group to conceive, but I watched her celebrate with great joy when others conceived. She also became an instrument of God to help others struggling with their inability to conceive. This book is an outgrowth of the wonderful work she is doing.

Helen is extremely transparent in a most personal and private way. You can actually feel her pain and her anguish as you read through the pages of this manual. Although she struggled with the desire to conceive, God used her to help other women learn how to T.R.U.S.T. in Him who is able to do "exceedingly abundantly above all we could ever ask or think." Helen helps other women learn that only total surrender to the will of God for their lives will help them deal with the hurt they feel when they so desperately want to conceive, and conception seems more like an illusion than a possibility.

She challenges women to take off the mask, and allow others to see and feel your hurts as you journey through the wilderness of barrenness. Even though it's risky, and you must be careful with whom you share your innermost feelings, it is the only way others can share in your pain and help you realize that you are not alone.

I highly recommend this book to everyone. Husbands can gain much insight into the struggles their wives endure when they want to conceive, and cannot. Hannah's husband, Elkanah did not understand her struggles and therefore was not as compassionate as he could have been. He asked her, "Hannah, why do you weep? Why do you not eat? And why is your heart grieved? Am I not better to you than ten sons?" He didn't get it and many of our husbands don't get it. As badly as he wanted to see her happy he did not understand that she would not be fulfilled as long as her womb was fruitless.

This book is not only for women who are barren or who struggle with infertility; it is also for individuals who need to learn that obstacles in our lives. No matter how large and overwhelming they may be, you can overcome if we put our trust in God. When we seek His face God, through prayer and fasting, will hear us and bless us. You will be able to experience God in an intimate way and He will give you the assurance that "You Are Not Alone."

Beulah R. Glover
Minister/School Administrator
Mount Bethel Ministries
Mount Bethel Christian Academy

INTRODUCTION
My Journey

I found myself dealing with one of the most difficult emotions, rejection! Since rejection wouldn't be enough, I decided to add hurt, anger, and frustration to the list of emotions that consumed me. I cried out to God and said, "I am tired of living behind the mask. I am tired of pretending to be happy when I am not. I am tired of pretending to have it all together when I don't." It was at this point that the healing began. I was invited to a Women's Retreat the weekend of April 12 - 15, 2007. This retreat enabled me to learn true forgiveness. Prior to learning forgiveness, I walked around angry at the world.

I walked around with anger against my church because I felt they didn't respond to our need when our roof collapsed, which left us displaced for six weeks. I was angry with my husband. I was angry at the administration of my school. I was angry, angry, and angrier. I went to church each Sunday carrying this anger back and forth. I knew when to stand, clap, wave my hand, and say Amen. I wore my mask securely in place Sunday after Sunday. I pretended week after week at work. I pretended month after month at our TRUST meetings. I felt that God had called me to be a leader and leaders have it together. My feeling was as a Christian leader, I couldn't let anyone know I had marital problems. I definitely couldn't let them know that there was no joy in my job. I am ashamed to admit that I was faking it as though I was making it. I realize now that I was only fooling myself. It was during this Sonshine Via De Cristo Retreat that I responded to the Holy Spirit and let go and forgave. As a result, I felt free for the first time in years. Matthew 18:21 NKJV "Lord, how often shall my brother sin against me, and I forgive him? Up to seven times?"

"Excellence is to do a common thing in an uncommon way." *Booker T. Washington*

PART I

PURSUIT

Depart from evil and do good; Seek peace and pursue it.
~ Psalm 34:14 NKJV

My husband's first thought of Pursuit is you are going after something. My friend Gloria said her first thought was to passionately hunt down. The Merriam-Webster Dictionary definition of Pursuit is the act of pursuing; endeavor to attain; occupation, employment

What is your pursuit? I find that our pursuit often depends on where we are in life. I was carefree during my high school years as my pursuit was my diploma. I look back at that time of life when my only responsibility was attending school, studying, and getting good grades. I graduated from Miami Northwestern Senior High School in the class of 1984, #41 in a class of 381. Once I graduated my pursuit became obtaining my degree in Elementary Education while I matriculated at Bethune-Cookman College. Though I was challenged with passing the Math part of the CLAST exam and was delayed a few years, I graduated in April 1991 with my Bachelor of Science Degree. Next, my pursuit was obtaining a teaching job. I started my teaching career in Palm Beach County as a third grade teacher in 1991. I also had a pursuit to meet Mr.

Right, which then led to a pursuit of a family. I met Jeff at Mt. Bethel Baptist Church in May 1995. We married the following year in December. It was the next pursuit that I found myself stagnant. I had set goals and obtained each of them until it came to the goal of having children. We were in a season of wait for seven years and eight months. Family, friends and many well-wishers told us just relax, or have you considered adoption? It is easier said than done. My present pursuit is to meet and encourage as many couples as I can through this book. It is possible to have more than one pursuit at a time. For example, my son Jeffrey, ensuring his happiness, safety and health is always a pursuit along with my husband, family, friends, T. R. U. S. T. and personal projects that GOD has given me. The bible encourages us to first seek (pursue) Christ and his righteousness and everything else will be added to us. Matthew 6:33 But seek first the kingdom of God and His righteousness, and all these things shall be added to you.

HOW ARE YOU COPING?

It can be a difficult time when you are in a season of waiting for a child at any given moment. There is no rhyme or reason as to what may set off an emotional landslide. It can be a comment made in passing or even the lack of one when needed the most. There were a number of different things that would get me thinking. My husband often tells me that I am very analytical and I rip apart the simplest thing in a matter of milliseconds. Unfortunately, he is correct. The thought of me not enjoying or appreciating some things that have crossed my path because I was so busy trying to figure it out is disheartening. It made me re-evaluate how I process things. It was not a great picture that was painted of me when it came to my reaction to people and circumstances around me.

I had to truly pray and ask GOD for help! Have you ever gone to an event with everything in place from the top of your head to the soles of your feet, but everything inside is out of place? One of my most difficult struggles was the reaction of others. It did not matter the location or the caliber of people. It happened in the pews at church, the teacher's lounge, the hair salon, as well as family reunions. I had several people look me in the eye and ask, "So do you want kids?" or "Why are you waiting so long to start a family?" My dear friend Bev told me to reply with "When God is ready." I soon learned that some people still inquired beyond that. It appeared the more evasive I was the deeper they delve not realizing the pain their questions inflicted. I appeared to always have it together, but I was crying silent tears. God inspired me to begin the ministry TRUST (Totally Relinquishing Unto our Savior Today and Tomorrow) to minister to women hurting from infertility issues. Shortly after the first meeting, I was invited to a baby shower. God blessed me to genuinely be happy for the honoree. I was asked while at the baby shower "How do you continue to come to other people's baby showers and act like you are having a good time?" I responded with "I am, if I cannot be happy for my sister how will I expect someone else to be happy for me when my time comes. Through prayer and fasting, God allowed me to minister to others during my season of waiting. It wasn't easy but it was during those times that my prayer life became stronger and stronger. I would go to God in prayer with my raw feelings and lay them all before him. It was during those times that I felt validated because God didn't judge me. He listened and comforted me. He gave me the strength to seek his word and stand on it and Trust Him. It was during this season that my favorite scripture became, Trust in the LORD with all your heart, and lean not on your own understanding; In all your ways acknowledge Him, And He shall direct your paths. Proverbs 3:5-6 NKJV. I had to trust Him when the doctors told me something contrary to what I wanted to hear. I had to trust Him when I felt my husband, family, or friends didn't understand my feelings. I had to Trust Him when the storms of life began to rage and I didn't feel strong enough to stand through them. I praise God because I am still standing on that Trust in Him.

DID I DREAM THAT?

While in Naples, celebrating our sixth anniversary, in December 2002, I had a dream of our son. I shared the dream with my husband of how I saw our son dressed in a vest, but I couldn't tell what kind of function we were attending. He said, "He was dressed like that because he is a King's kid." This dream encouraged me until the next month when I received the physical sign that I was not pregnant. I wept once again because it meant another month to wait and hope that there wouldn't be a cycle. Then I wondered did I really dream that I saw our son, or could it have been my emotions once again getting the best of me? I wanted to be a mother so bad that there were times that I felt I was pregnant because I was feeling all the signs of a pregnant woman. I praise God because He reigns! As Christians, we are to be "Light" wherever we go. I knew deep down that God was speaking to me through my dream and we would have our promised child. All I had to do was believe, no matter what.

It was during that season that my faith grew. I remembered what God shared with me in that dream and I encouraged myself through those seasons of waiting. If God has given you assurance through a prayer, a dream, or a spoken word; believe what He told you no matter how the circumstances may appear. I didn't focus on the dream of fighting against darkness. I chose to focus on "light" and God's promise to us. I took the second dream as a warning to continue to Trust God and praise Him regardless of what I faced.

ANOTHER MONTH?

There were quite a few times that I would feel so down when I received my menstrual cycle. I was certain that I was pregnant. Upon receiving, my menstrual cycle it was devastating. I remember getting in a fetal position and just weeping. During my weeping I would think of how I wanted my miracle now! I would wonder how much longer I had to wait. There were moments that I felt so low that I could not express my feelings. There were times when I tried to pray, but could not.

My most recent trial was no cycle at all. My antennas went up and I began to calculate when I had my last cycle. As each day came and went without a cycle I got more and more excited. I took five home pregnancy tests and they were all negative. I was then scheduled for a blood test through my primary care physician. Those were the longest twenty-four hours to wait for the results. I went numb when I called and was told, "Mrs. King it was negative, keep trying." I fought hard to keep the tears at bay. I didn't know it could still hurt so bad to find out that I was not pregnant. Then, the responsibility of sharing the bad news with my husband was overwhelming. We both then wonder why I was two weeks late and had no cycle. The results of my ultrasound revealed that I had a cyst along with fibroid tumors. My doctor wanted me to repeat the ultrasound to monitor the cyst a week after my next cycle was to begin. I was in a strange place because I still did not have a cycle. Then I was told that this could be a sign of the beginning of menopause. The finality of that was also overwhelming but I stood on Proverbs 3:5-6 NKJV states, Trust in the LORD with all your heart, and lean not on your own understanding; In all your ways acknowledge Him And He shall direct your paths.

Where has your journey taken you? It really amazed me some of the requests that are made when seeing an infertility specialist. I could not believe it when we were told to have sexual relations, not shower and come into the office to be examined. It was one of the hardest requests to follow, but because we wanted the promised results, we did it. I must admit that I did some unorthodox things as suggested by others in order to try to conceive. I am not pleased that I also took Robitussin when I didn't have a cold because it was said to build up a woman's cervical mucus. I even went as far as holding my buttocks and legs in the air to make sure the sperm was able to swim down. It often amazed me, the two most famous lines that people often told me were "Relax and not think about it and then it will happen." Or "Have you considered adoption?" "I know a sister who adopted and then she found out she was pregnant." This is why God has instructed that we are to seek Godly counsel in order to avoid humiliating memories like a few I have shared. If you are honest, you may have some similar memories of things you thought would bring you the results that you so desired.

DOES HE HAVE A CLUE?

There were times throughout the process I felt my husband was clueless to what I was really feeling. It appeared no matter how many times, or what depth I shared; he was still oblivious to the magnitude of it all. This often baffled me because he was by my side for many of the procedures. He experienced the mood swings first hand, yet there were times when he appeared as if it was all new to him. I learned that he dealt with his disappointments internally. I, on the other hand, wanted to talk about it to share my feelings and gauge his feelings. My method wasn't often reciprocated which left us feeling at odds. There were several nights that I was up on the Internet researching more information on whatever our latest assignment was from the doctor. It amazed me how my husband could sleep when we had an upcoming procedure scheduled.

Ladies, please know that your husband does care and he does support you. I am speaking from personal experience of frustration when Jeff didn't respond the way I wanted him to respond. Seek God during these times and He will comfort you.

Also having the support of TRUST gave me comfort because I was able to call one of my sisters in Christ and share what I was feeling and we would encourage each other.

LEARNING TO T. R. U. S. T.

Throughout my process and desiring to have my own child, I learned to trust GOD. There were several moments that I felt like I was triumphing as well plummeting. I learned to have my own praise period at home. It also increased the time that I now spend in prayer, fasting, bible study and meditation.

Scriptures that Comfort

Proverbs 3:5-6
Romans 8:37-39
Isaiah 55:11
Psalm 128:3
Matthew 17:20

IS SOMETHING REALLY WRONG WITH ME?

I recall, now, what struggle really is. Struggle is getting your husband to do a semen analysis. This had to be the largest struggle I've encountered within this aspect of my marriage. Years passed before he finally consented. However, he received a positive result. He was told that he could be a sperm donor because his sperm count was so high. While I celebrated with him the reality set in that if it wasn't him then there was something wrong with me. I began to carry the burden that it was my inadequacy as a woman that prevented us from having a child. That was a huge burden to carry. My self-esteem plummeted to an all time low. As it set in, the weight became immense while I meditated in my reasoning that I was the reason for our fertility issues. I became obsessed with trying whatever medical intervention I could to fix me. My doctor put me on a low dosage of Clomid to start me off. I demanded more Clomid thinking that would fix the problem. My doctor explained that studies have shown one of the side effects of Clomid is that women who were on it for long periods of time have been diagnosed with uterine cancer. I didn't care about the risk at that time I just wanted to do whatever I thought would work to get me pregnant. She suggested I see an infertility specialist after a few months when the Clomid didn't work. Have you ever felt like doing something that could harm you medically just to have a baby?

I know the pain of wanting to conceive so bad that you are willing to try anything. It bothered me when people told me to relax and to not think about it then it would happen. I was screaming inside because their words were unrealistic for me, because I never relaxed. There was not a moment that I didn't think about it. I carried it with me everywhere I went. I admired babies and pregnant women. I longed to be pregnant. It is a strong desire that if not dealt with can be overwhelming. I chose to deal with my desire through prayer and connecting with the ladies of TRUST. This support group helped me feel validated and not give up.

TICK TOCK

Have you ever just sat and listened to the sound a clock makes? Tick tock. The sound is deafening as each second turns into a minute. Then each minute turns into another minute. There have been times that the clock on the wall is ticking so loud that I feel it's a part of my body. Yes with each tick tock, my heart pounds as my mind races. The clock ticked loudly as I waited to hear the results of a pregnancy test from the doctor. Tick tock. As I dialed the doctor's office to receive the results. Tick Tock as the phone rings. Once they finally answer, they place you on hold to get your results. Tick tock it seems like forever before they return to the phone. Tick tock. It seems like time stops as you wait for the results.

There was also the time that I went through the Intrauterine Insemination (IUI) cycle and was told in two weeks you will know if it worked. If you don't get your cycle it worked. If you get your cycle the chances are it didn't work. Tick tock. Those were two of the longest weeks of my life. I would look at the clock only to see that only five minutes had gone by. Tick tock. Then I would allow myself to get happy and dream of baby blue or pink. What would our child look like? When would my due date be? Who would we tell first? How long do we wait to tell? Whoa, I need to calm down because there is a possibility that I am not pregnant. The emotional roller coaster would start again. There were highs and lows the entire two weeks of waiting. Then, the dreaded day came when it's time for the cycle. I thought OH NO! You were not supposed to come on! I am supposed to be pregnant! The egg on the screen was a perfect round one. What happened? Why didn't the IUI work? The tears flowed again! Why am I crying when I knew there was a chance that it wouldn't work? How do I tell Jeff that it didn't work? It is once again my responsibility to share the sad news. Then I decide that we will just do it again. I make the decision to try another IUI next month. I take out the calendar and chart the next time we can perform the IUI. I didn't consult GOD. I didn't consult my husband. I have become obsessed with being pregnant. The infertility specialist said this is a good option for us since I have one blocked tube. This is the best method for us. After I charted it, called the office, and planned it out; I finally decided to consult my husband only to find out that day is not good for him. What do you mean it's not good for you? The calendar says this is when I am ovulating and this is the best time. We were so close last time. I then decide that I will take my husband's semen in a jar with me and have the procedure done. I give it some thought and feel it is a good plan. My husband sat and looked at me lovingly (I am sure praying for direction) as to how to handle me with care. I made the plans without him and want him to follow them. He gently reminds me that we agreed that he would drive me to the procedure and back home. Once back home I am off my feet for the next 24 hours to relax and allow nature to take its course. He doesn't feel it's a good idea for me to drive myself. TICK TOCK, Tick tock. Time is standing still as I try to process what he is saying. Tick tock. Time is standing still as he holds his breath awaiting my response. There is silence. I go into the bathroom to have a good cry because he obviously doesn't understand how important this is and I call out to GOD. GOD gently reminds me that He has been waiting for me to come to Him. He reminds me that He knew me before I was formed in my mother's womb. I am humbled at God's loving response to my asking Him why it didn't work. God led me to the scripture Matthew 6:33 NKJV which states, But seek first the kingdom of God and His righteousness, and all these things shall be added to you. I cried again, but this time peace began to hold me and cuddle me like I was in a safe cocoon.

PART II

BE STILL AND KNOW

The LORD will fight for you, and you shall hold your peace." ~ Exodus 14:14 NKJV

    God desires that we repent our sins and surrender our lives to Him and be careful to allow Him to teach us. God loves us and desires for us to seek Godly wisdom and counsel through prayer and fasting. Prayer is one of the greatest privileges ever given to God's people. Jeremiah 33:3 NKJV states, 'Call to Me, and I will answer you, and show you great and mighty things, which you do not know.' Prayer is an obligation to every Christian that should be as natural as breathing. However, prayer does not always bring instant results. 2 Chronicles 7:14 NKJV states, if My people who are called by My name will humble themselves, and pray and seek My face, and turn from their wicked ways, then I will hear from heaven, and will forgive their sin and heal their land. God wants us to have confidence in him because he has all power. I was blessed by an email and I no longer look at the acronym ASAP the same. It used to make me feel overwhelmed because of another demand. ASAP stands for Always Say a Prayer. Psalm 46:10 NKJV states, Be still, and know that I am God; I will be exalted among the nations, I will be exalted in the earth! We have to learn to saturate ourselves with the word of God; replace lies with truth of the word of God. Philippians 3:13-14 NKJV states, Brethren, I do not count myself to have apprehended; but one thing I do, forgetting those things which are behind and reaching forward to those things which are ahead, I press toward the goal for the prize of the upward call of God in Christ Jesus. The prize, which God has called me heavenward in Christ Jesus. Real praise is being able to praise God regardless of our circumstances. True praise comes from our relationship with God. You cannot praise God if you do not know God. We must stay in constant communion with God. It is those difficult times, which cause us to go slower which causes us to open our introspection to new capacities. Do not delay going to the next level by refusing to praise Him. If you sit long enough God will reveal His plan for your life. Satan knows that we can't know God if we are rushing here and there. We must spend quality time in prayer fasting, and praise. No matter what is going on in my life God will get the glory. 2 Chronicles 20:15 NKJV states, And he said, "Listen, all you of Judah and you inhabitants of Jerusalem, and you, King Jehoshaphat! Thus says the LORD to you: 'Do not be afraid nor dismayed because of this great multitude, for the battle is not yours, but God's. God is in the midst of it all. God is our shepherd. He is in front of us. He is behind us. He is all around us. All day and all night the angels are watching over us. God wants us to be quiet; turn the TV and radio off sit before Him in the quietness of His presence.

RENEWING OF YOUR MIND

Do not conform any longer to the pattern of this world, but be transformed by the renewing of your mind. Then you will be able to test and approve what God's will is his good, pleasing perfect will. ~ Romans 12:2 NIV

We need to expand our minds. God is the source of our peace beyond our understanding. No matter what we do or where we go, the Lord is there! The more time we spend in prayer, the more we understand who God really is. The more time we spend with God the more power we have. More prayer – more power. No prayer – no power. We need to establish some time on a daily basis to spend time with the lover of our souls. We must learn to set the atmosphere in order that it is conducive for us being in His presence as we seek God for answers to our struggles. We need to call the names out, as they are in order to get into your spirit. We know that God is a comforter. We also know he gives us peace and joy. God is able to give us what we need when we earnestly seek Him. Adjectives for seek: look for, search, inquire, desire. 2 Chronicles 15:2 NKJV states, And he went out to meet Asa, and said to him: "Hear me, Asa, and all Judah and Benjamin. The LORD is with you while you are with Him. If you seek Him, He will be found by you; but if you forsake Him, He will forsake you. Hebrews 11:6 NKJV states, But without faith it is impossible to please Him, for he who comes to God must believe that He is, and that He is a rewarder of those who diligently seek Him. Prayer is an experience of waiting. We have to be determined not to give up and not be depressed while we are waiting. We need to keep making deposits of God's word into our spirit in order for it that it spills over into our emotions. If we do not put anything in we cannot get anything out. We need to renew our minds because it all begins with a thought. It is how we respond or react to the thought that determines whether or not it will manifest into something more. Next the thought is spoken. Finally the thought becomes an action. This is why we have to be careful about what thoughts we allow to linger because it can turn into something more than we desire. God's delays are not God's refusals. I John 1:9 states, if we confess our sins, He is faithful and just and will forgive us our sins and purify us from all unrighteousness. Peace is not about our circumstances being changed but about us changing. God loves us enough that He wants to repair us so we don't go to the new place with the old stuff. When God gives the promise, God has already made the provision. God's delays are not necessarily God's denial. God allows us to wait, so He can repair us in order to prepare us for His answer. God does not answer us immediately because God is waiting for our will to line up with God's will. We had to wait 7 years and 8 months to conceive. There were many times that I had to renew my mind and my way of thinking. I chose to be positive, celebrate with others as well as spend time and invest in my nieces and nephews while waiting on my promised child. I did not allow thoughts of anger and jealousy to linger and take a bitter root. I encourage you to do the same as you wait. There are several organizations where you can volunteer as well as donate your time. Pray and ask God to strengthen you to be able to support someone else as you wait to receive your manifestation.

DROUGHT

Merriam-Webster Dictionary states, Drought: (1) a period of dryness especially when prolonged; one that causes extensive damage to crops or prevents their successful growth. (2) a prolonged or chronic shortage or lack of something expected or desired. The Britannica Online Encyclopedia states, "Drought is the most serious physical hazard to agriculture in nearly every part of the world. Efforts have been made to control it by seeding clouds to induce rainfall but those experiments have only limited success."

There are four basic types of drought[1]. Permanent drought, which is impossible without continuous irrigation. Seasonal drought, that which is planted must be adjusted so that crops develop during the rainy season. Unpredictable drought is abnormal rainfall failure; it usually affects only a relatively small area. Invisible drought showers may not supply enough water to restore the amount lost.

1. **<u>Permanent Drought</u>** - If you had an opportunity to write a farewell letter to your loved

---

[1] Four basic types of drought topics, The Britannica Online Encyclopedia
Thoughts for the four basic types of drought, by Helen King

ones, what would it say? If you knew like the miners in the mining accident a couple years ago that Your death was inevitable, what words would you leave them to remember you? 9/11/2001 will always be a life changing day for me. I often think about the people who got up and conducted business as usual, but they did not know they would never return home. I thought about the man who stopped for a bandage because his new shoes hurt; which saved his life. My goal is to let those who are most important to me know that I love them, not only through words, but taking the time to mail a card or phone them. You see I have cards for friends that I never mailed. I have thought of a person but not followed through with a phone call.

2. **Seasonal Drought** - God is the Great Physician. It is for our benefit to study and read God's word so it is with us at all times. There will be times when you will be challenged and may not have your physical bible in your hand, but you are able to recall a scripture that will bring you encouragement and strengthen you to make it through that situation. For example, the morning of September 21, 2005, I was scheduled to have my son Jeffrey via c-section. Right before delivering they could not hear his heartbeat. Jeff was standing outside the room with no idea what was happening inside the operating room. I had the anesthesiologist

and nurse right above me having a conversation about not hearing anything when my doctor said, "Helen what side do we usually hear his (I didn't catch that until later that he referred to him as his) heartbeat. I immediately went into prayer mode and began praying God's word back to Him. "Lord you did not give me a spirit of fear, but of power, love and of sound mind. Lord you did not bring me this far to leave me. You gave me this child and you are sovereign and will allow this child to bring you glory." I didn't know Jeff had come back into the room until he kissed me and touched my face because I had closed my eyes and shut out everyone around me in order to use my faith and pray! We all know the end result was God blessing us with a 7 lb 9 oz healthy baby boy! Once again, I did not allow thoughts of fear to linger and make me doubt instead I chose to be positive and pray.

3. **Unpredictable Drought** - In James 4:13-17 NIV just to paraphrase states, that we often make plans and go about what we plan to do but its best to say "If it is the Lord's will. James 5:7-11 NIV is also a powerful read. Both of these scriptures challenge us to maintain a close walk with God, so when we find ourselves in an unpredictable place we don't panic.

On December 14, 2007 I decided (I didn't pray

about it) not to take Jeffrey home, but to do something fun with him. It was my initial PLAN to take him to the movies. We arrived at 4pm only to find out that Alvin and the Chipmunks didn't start until 5:15pm. I didn't want to wait for over an hour with a two year old, therefore we left and went to Miami Subs. I thought then, we can go back to the theater because once we eat it will be closer to the time for the movie. I thought, "Hmmm, I am close to the beach I will let him go wet his feet." The thought of the movie still lingered, but I ignored it. I went to the beach because that is a free and fun thing to do. We went and we were robbed when someone broke my window out. However, God was still sovereign with the first Good Samaritan walked the beach to find the owner, which gave me the opportunity to call the bank and cancel my checking account. The second set of good Samaritans was two ladies who happened to be at the beach taking holiday photos. They were nice enough to wait with me until the police arrived. Those ladies did not leave me alone, and they gave me free usage of their cell phones. Jeffrey was calm the entire time sitting in his car seat.

What has God told you to do on the east side, but you keep going on the west? Please allow my example to lead you to seek Him. God does want us to seek Him about ALL things. Something as simple as should I take my son to the beach for a free afternoon cost us $250.00 for a new window, time needed to replace my drivers' license, loss of precious photos and the physical list could go on, but my challenge to you is what will it cost you to be OBEDIENT and go in the direction that you know He is calling you. Joshua 1:6-7 NKJV states, Be strong and of good courage, for to this people you shall divide as an inheritance the land which I swore to their fathers to give them. Only be strong and very courageous, that you may observe to do according to all the law which Moses My servant commanded you; do not turn from it to the right hand or to the left, that you may prosper wherever you go.

4. **<u>Invisible Drought</u>** - When I initially woke up I checked on Jeffrey and he was sleeping peacefully. Then an hour and 20 minutes later he cried out for me because he was soaked and wet. I had to change him and allow him to lay on my chest as I finished writing. As a parent, I have to make decisions as it relates to our son.

I don't know all the answers and often seek the advice of other parents for different situations. Well, it's the same with God. He is our heavenly father and has so much to share and give to us, but we don't always seek Him.

This is what God gave me for Invisible "Where is the leash?" I read a story about a man who trained his dog to carry his leash in his mouth to be in accordance with the local law when all dogs must be on a leash. Those around him were amazed when the dog didn't run off, but walked right beside his owner even when they passed a cat. He didn't run off to chase the cat. The writer stated that isn't it awesome that even though God has an invisible leash[2] on all of us that He doesn't yank it to get our attention or snatch on it. That was powerful for me because there have been times when I have chosen to do things my way and I end up falling and having to go back and seek God because things didn't work as I expected. It is better to seek God for His will rather than trying to figure it out and do it on our own.

CLUTTER

Clutter can really distract us from being on point where God desires for us to be. Psalm 55:22 NKJV states, Cast your burden on the LORD, And He shall sustain you; He shall never permit the righteous to be moved.

A person's closet usually tells you a lot about the individual. For example, for many years I had several sizes

---

[2] Our Daily Bread, March 8, 2008, RBC Ministries/Discovery House Publishers, Grand Rapids, MI 49501

in my closet with the belief that I would get back down to a certain size again, or I would hold onto the larger ones just in case I needed them.

I. Secret:

All of us need at least one or two friends. A friend is someone who knows all about your secrets, but still likes you the same[3]. I once read that you can choose your friends, but not your family. It is powerful when a friendship goes through a major episode and survives it. If you are looking for faults to correct, try looking in the mirror. The grandmother of my childhood friend Michele told me, "Helen whatever you do as long as you can look at yourself in the mirror you will be fine." Mrs. Ruby's words never left me and I think of them often when it comes to making choices that could do major damage to my reputation. I want to look at myself in the mirror knowing I chose to do something without shame.

II. Clutter:

What is on your to do list? Is it cleaning out an overstuffed closet? Organizing the kitchen cabinets? Paying your monthly bills? When do you plan to get it done?

---

[3] Our Daily Bread, March 8, 2008, RBC Ministries/Discovery House Publishers, Grand Rapids, MI 49501

While a to-do-list is helpful, another type of list is even more valuable: a "To Be" list. Albert Einstein said, "Try not to become a man of value but to be a value to someone." What are your family and friends able to say about you with regards to how you handle your season of waiting? Are you bitter and angry? Does your husband walk on eggshells around you because he is unsure how you may respond at any given moment? Are you known for being fragile? Do you allow God to receive the glory by still having joy through your pain? Do you encourage others even though you are hurting?

III. Valuables:

Sometimes God doesn't answer our prayer requests right away. After time elapses we begin to feel like the psalmist who said, "How long, O Lord? Will you forget me forever? Psalm 13:1 NIV. I remember feeling like that on one occasion while waiting on results from procedures. Do you put your time and energy into material possessions instead of into your salvation, which cannot be taken away from you? The most valuable thing you can give to anyone is Christ. Are you willing to offer Christ to family, friends, and co-workers? Are you willing to teach them the ABCs, which are **A**ccept Jesus, **B**elieve in Him, and **C**onfess your sins.

TRANSITION

Your servant Joab did this to change the present situation. My lord has wisdom like that of an angel of God--he knows everything that happens in the land. ~ 2 Samuel 14:20 NIV

Merriam-Webster Dictionary states, Transition: a passage from one state, stage subject, or place to another

I. Under New Management

We receive the gift of the indwelling spirit who intends to put our entire life under "new management" in order to transition us to the place God called us to be. God is looking for willing participants who fully believe and agree that life under His control is better than under the old management. The new management seeks to transition us from the destructive patterns of old desires to the new management style which entails peace, love, joy and happiness to name a few. However, under the new management we are sometimes challenged to make radical choices. 2 Samuel 15:15 NIV states, The King's officials answered him, "Your servants are ready to do whatever our Lord the King chooses." "Management by Jesus" should be the sign that hangs on all our lives. . . .

II. Where do we go from here?

Is there a relative, a friend, sister or a brother in Christ with whom you need to make things right? Then why not do it today? Allow God to heal you as you release yourself from carrying the burden. Once we decide to accept Jesus as our Lord and Savior we must actively work on the transition of following him at all cost. Daniel 2:21 NIV states, He changes times and seasons; he sets up Kings and deposes them. He gives wisdom to the wise and knowledge to the discerning.

III. Abrupt Changes

    A. Natural disaster
    B. Death
    C. Job change/relocation
    D. Baby

Leviticus 26:4 NIV states, I will send you rain in its season, and the ground will yield its crops and the trees of the field their fruit. In every transition it is good to look both ways. When Joshua assumed leadership of Israel, God told him to consider the past and the future: "Moses My servant is dead. Now therefore, arise, go over this Jordan you and all this people, to the land which I am giving to them" (Joshua 1:2 NKJV). Then He promised, "As I was with Moses, so I will be with you. . . . . Do not be afraid, nor be dismayed for the Lord your God is with you wherever you go." (vv5, 9). Therefore with confidence in God, we can look back then forward and walk boldly into a new era that God is sending us. Numbers 13:20 NKJV states, whether the land *is* rich or poor; and whether there are forests there or not. Be of good courage. And bring some of the fruit of the land." Now the time *was* the season of the first ripe grapes.

In Matthew 4:18-22 NKJV, [18] And Jesus, walking by the Sea of Galilee, saw two brothers, Simon called Peter, and Andrew his brother, casting a net into the sea; for they were fishermen. [19] Then He said to them, "Follow Me, and I will make you fishers of men." [20] They immediately left their nets and followed Him. [21] Going on from there, He saw two other brothers, James *the son* of Zebedee, and John his brother, in the boat with Zebedee their father, mending their nets. He called them, [22] and immediately they left the boat and their father, and followed Him.

Questions to ponder. . .

The New King James Version Jesus transitions His followers from fish to people. What would be different in your relationships if people were more important than your self-interests?

Is there something that Jesus asks you to do today that is risky? Can you trust him?

Who knows more about life challenges, you or Jesus? If your answer is Jesus, why are you still trying to manage your own life on your own terms?

CORE

And we know that all things work together for good to those who love God, to those who are the called according to His purpose. ~ Romans 8:28 NKJV

The Wizard of Oz[4] had four main characters. **Dorothy**, whose goal was to find her way **home**. The **Scarecrow** desired a **brain**. Next, the **Tin Man** longed for a **heart**. Lastly, the **Lion** wanted **courage**. Let's look at each character separately and collectively. The movie also had some other characters that had pivotal roles. Those characters were the Wicked Witch of the West and of course the Wizard of Oz.

Dorothy's goal was to find her way home. As Christians our ultimate goal is to make it to heaven with our Lord and Savior Jesus Christ. All of our actions should reflect that goal. The film portrayed Dorothy as a carefree young lady who lived with her aunt and uncle until her dog Toto was threatened to be taken away for biting. Dorothy thought it best to run away with Toto from the situation.

Let's pause here to ponder that thing that GOD has called us to do. Did we run away? Was it easier to veer to

---

[4] The Wizard of Oz, Noel Langley and Florence Ryerson, (Metro-Goldwyn-Mayer (MGM) 1939)

the left or right when He told us to remain on the path? I thought it interesting that Dorothy's character did everything she was told in order to get back home when in fact she ran away from that very place. Let's make it more personal for this ministry, TRUST that is for women desiring to have children. What have we done along the path of our yellow brick road in order to become a mother? What feelings have we dealt with along the journey? Did you ever get weary? Read Isaiah 40:28-31 NKJV [28] Have you not known? Have you not heard? The everlasting God, the LORD, The Creator of the ends of the earth, Neither faints nor is weary. His understanding is unsearchable. [29] He gives power to the weak, And to *those who have* no might He increases strength. [30] Even the youths shall faint and be weary, And the young men shall utterly fall, [31] But those who wait on the LORD Shall renew *their* strength; They shall mount up with wings like eagles, They shall run and not be weary, They shall walk and not faint.

Scarecrow desired a brain. As Christians we are taught to pray about ALL things and encouraged to seek GODLY counsel. The scarecrow throughout the movie displayed intelligence along the path of the yellow brick road. However, because he couldn't physically show his brain he felt he lacked it. I feel it's that way with faith, because we can't see it but we must believe that GOD is able. Hebrews 11:1 NKJV states, Now faith is the substance of things hoped for, the evidence of things not seen. Although chapter 11 of Hebrew gives us many examples of faith we have other examples. Who is it that you can identify with from the bible? Is it the widow who was preparing her last meal when she was told to give it to the prophet? I Kings 17:12-15 NKJV So she said, "As the LORD your God lives, I do not have bread, only a handful of flour in a bin, and a little oil in a jar; and see, I *am* gathering a couple of sticks that I may go in and prepare it for myself and my son, that we may eat it, and die." **13** And Elijah said to her, "Do not fear; go *and* do as you have said, but make me a small cake from it first, and bring *it* to me; and afterward make *some* for yourself and your son. **14** For thus says the LORD God of Israel: 'The bin of flour shall not be used up, nor shall the jar of oil run dry, until the day the LORD sends rain on the earth.'" **15** So she went away and did according to the word of Elijah; and she and he and her household ate for *many* days.

Is it Hannah who continued to go to the temple to pray? I Samuel 1:10-27 NKJV **10** And she *was* in bitterness of soul, and prayed to the LORD and wept in anguish. **11** Then she made a vow and said, "O LORD of hosts, if You will indeed look on the affliction of Your maidservant and remember me, and not forget Your maidservant, but will give Your maidservant a male child, then I will give him to the LORD all the days of his life, and no razor shall come upon his head." **12** And it happened, as she continued praying before the LORD, that Eli watched her mouth. **13** Now Hannah spoke in her heart; only her lips moved, but her voice was not heard. Therefore

Eli thought she was drunk. **14** So Eli said to her, "How long will you be drunk? Put your wine away from you!" **15** But Hannah answered and said, "No, my lord, I *am* a woman of sorrowful spirit. I have drunk neither wine nor intoxicating drink, but have poured out my soul before the LORD. **16** Do not consider your maidservant a wicked woman, for out of the abundance of my complaint and grief I have spoken until now." **17** Then Eli answered and said, "Go in peace, and the God of Israel grant your petition which you have asked of Him." **18** And she said, "Let your maidservant find favor in your sight." So the woman went her way and ate, and her face was no longer *sad.* **19** Then they rose early in the morning and worshiped before the LORD, and returned and came to their house at Ramah. And Elkanah knew Hannah his wife, and the LORD remembered her. **20** So it came to pass in the process of time that Hannah conceived and bore a son, and called his name Samuel, *saying,* "Because I have asked for him from the LORD."
21 Now the man Elkanah and all his house went up to offer to the LORD the yearly sacrifice and his vow. **22** But Hannah did not go up, for she said to her husband, "*Not* until the child is weaned; then I will take him, that he may appear before the LORD and remain there forever."
23 So Elkanah her husband said to her, "Do what seems best to you; wait until you have weaned him. Only let the LORD establish His word." Then the woman stayed and nursed her son until she had weaned him. **24** Now when she had weaned him, she took him up with her, with three bulls, one ephah of flour, and a skin of wine, and brought

him to the house of the LORD in Shiloh. And the child *was* young. [25] Then they slaughtered a bull, and brought the child to Eli. [26] And she said, "O my lord! As your soul lives, my lord, I *am* the woman who stood by you here, praying to the LORD. [27] For this child I prayed, and the LORD has granted me my petition which I asked of Him.

It takes faith to pay your tithes. Malachi 3:10 NKJV states, Bring all the tithes into the storehouse, That there may be food in My house, And try Me now in this," Says the LORD of hosts, "If I will not open for you the windows of heaven And pour out for you such blessing That there will not be room enough to receive it. It takes faith to believe GOD for what he has shared with you in your quiet time. It took faith for me not to focus on what others would think when GOD gave me the vision for T. R. U. S. T. It took faith to continue with ministry when others were blessed with a pregnancy before me. What is GOD calling you to exercise your faith to do? Do you TRUST him?

Tin Man longed for a heart. The first time we accepted Jesus as our LORD and Savior we gained a new heart. Our new heart caused us to do things differently than we had in the past. The Tin Man longed to feel. As women we are emotional beings and we preface statements based on our emotions. However, we must learn not to rely on our feelings alone. There were times when I didn't feel like going or doing, and that was when I received my biggest blessings. If I had given in to how I felt I would have remained home and not pressed on and receive a life changing word. It is matters of the heart that often delay us. It's good to know that it's a delay and not a permanent place.

Lion wanted courage. The lion had more courage than he realized. He repeatedly acted courageously when they were faced with adversity along the path. As a Christian, it takes courage to stand and boldly allow GOD to use your life as an example to others. Ephesians 6:19 NKJV states, and for me, that utterance may be given to me, that I may open my mouth boldly to make known the mystery of the gospel. Each month I pray that GOD gives me courage to share with the ladies of TRUST whatever lesson that He has given me. I am presently serving on the prayer and caregiver's ministries at church. Those who know me well know that I am shy. However, it is hard for some people to believe that I am shy until I get to know a person. If I could, I would remain in the background. I believe in obedience, which is why I joined the prayer ministry. I had no problem praying on behalf of others needs privately or collectively. I thought I would just blend in, but GOD has allowed me to lead a prayer during our Saturday morning prayer. If the others could feel and hear my heart beat the first time I was called in front of the church to pray, they would have heard the loud thump. I accepted the call to join these ministries because it's what I do within TRUST anyway, pray and give care. However, I realize GOD has another plan for me. I am no longer able to hide behind others when I know GOD has petitioned me to be a leader.

My friend what has God called you do it? Does the assignment take you out of your comfort zone? Do you feel as if you are venturing to uncharted water? It is my advice to Trust God even when you cannot trace Him. I have learned that when I allow Him to lead me it is life changing.

The Wizard of Oz and the Wicked Witch of the West's goals were to control. The other two characters in the movies played their role as well. The Wizard of Oz stood in judgment of others when in fact he was dealing with his own issues. The Wizard of Oz turned out to be a phony because what appeared to be such a powerful empire really was just a lot of smoke. Does that sound familiar? Then, there is the Wicked Witch of the West who I immediately characterized with the same assignment that the enemy has which is to STOP or DETER us from our yellow brick road. GOD will give us the nuggets that we need to keep us on the path that He desires for us. We must be still and listen.

It has been stated that it takes 30 days to break or begin a habit. It is the belief that if one does the same act for 30 days straight it forms a habit. Are you willing to meet GOD at the same place and same time each day in order to form a daily habit of spending time with him? For me, my morning devotion goes well. It is my night offerings that fall short. It is my goal to spend time with Him each night before going to bed. I have learned to make myself accountable to my prayer partner in order to meet this goal. I learned last year at a women's retreat to just be silent and listen. I was guilty of praying but not taking the time to really listen to his answer. I didn't realize the magnitude of just being quiet and listening because I always have the TV or CD playing even if I am not actively engaged with what is on it. Now, I turn everything off and enjoy the quietness. GOD also desires for us to worship Him. My prayer partner taught me that worship begins at home. I was one of those people who waited until I got to church. Now I sing and have my own praise period at home.

The characters in this movie are like the body of Christ because once they came together they were able to accomplish collectively more than they could independently. Which character did you connect with? Do you like Dorothy want to get to a certain place? Are you the scarecrow looking in all the wrong places for what you already have or could it be the Tin Man wanting to feel? Do you have the courage like the lion to find out? Each of these characters had to get to the CORE of their individual desire. The Merriam-Webster Dictionary defines core as a central and often foundational part usually distinct from the enveloping part by a difference in nature. Core is a thing or place that is of greatest importance to an activity or interest. The Merriam-Webster Medical Dictionary states that core is the central part of a body, mass or part. In essence, core is the key element that we need to continuously evaluate in order to move forward in all aspects of our life.

PART III

Never Would Have Made It
Marvin Sapp[5]

Marvin Sapp's song *Never Would Have Made It* states it all. The song's lyrics go "Never could have made it without you. I would have lost my mind, I would have gave up, but you were right there, you were right there. I never could have made it without you. I am stronger. I am wiser. I am better, so much better. When I look back over what he brought me through I know I never could have made it. Never would have made it. Never could have made it without God.

Marvin Sapp encourages us to praise God through our trials regardless of what the circumstances are because it is God who sustains us.

Just a Prayer Away
Yolanda Adams[6]

I know that there are times in your life. When the wheels just seem to turn and uncertainties about your tomorrow seems to grow. One thing you should remember and you should always know, out of everyone who loves

---

[5] Marvin Sapp lyrics, Thirst – Verity Records 2007, Never Would Have Made It
[6] Yolanda Adams lyrics, Best of Yolanda Adams – Verity Records 1999, Just A Prayer Away

you I LOVE YOU THE MOST. For I am just a prayer away, call my name with your heart and I'll hear every word you say when you cry at night I'll wipe the tears away just pray my love I'll be there right away. You will never have to wonder about my love. Just put your faith and trust in my care I will always be there to hold you in my arms when you're afraid don't worry I'll protect you from the storm out of everyone who loves you I LOVE YOU THE MOST. I am just a prayer away call my name with your heart and I'll hear I am just a prayer away call my name with your heart and I'll hear I am just a prayer away call my name with your heart and I'll hear every word you say when you cry at night I'll wipe your tears away. Just pray my love I'll be there right away. I know that there are times in your life. When the wheels just seem to turn and uncertainties about your tomorrow seems to grow. One thing you should remember and you should always know, out of everyone who loves you I love you the most.

Psalm 51:1-2 NKJV states, Have mercy upon me, O God, According to Your lovingkindness; According to the multitude of Your tender mercies, Blot out my transgressions. Wash me thoroughly from my iniquity, And cleanse me from my sin.

ARE YOU READY FOR YOUR BREAKTHROUGH?

1. Are you prepared to accept Motherhood no matter what the cost?

There may be days when you don't feel your best. Will you complain or praise GOD through it? I was considered a high-risk pregnancy and had to go to the doctor twice a month. I continued to praise GOD even when I did not feel my best! I was diagnosed with Placenta Previa at twelve weeks and told that I could not have intercourse, travel, and I would possibly have bed rest. I prayed and asked GOD for strength daily. I used the information that the doctor gave me to direct my paths. My faith grew even more during this time because I believed with all my heart that God gave me this miracle pregnancy and He would sustain it regardless of what I was told was medically wrong. My doctor told me that I was high risk but I felt good and praised God for being able to walk, drive and work my entire pregnancy. God sustained me to carry our son full term without any complications. I praise God each time I look at my son because his presence in my life is a constant reminder of God's grace and mercy.

2. Are you willing to accept the bitter with the sweet?

As a mommy I can no longer give in to bad feelings. There is always something to be done. I have learned to praise GOD for my miracle and ask for strength and continue to move on. I prayed before conceiving and during pregnancy and that continues now as a Mother.

3. Have you considered how becoming a Mother will change your life forever?

    I thank GOD daily for blessing me with a healthy energetic baby boy. Jeffrey brings joy to my life daily. I look forward to picking him up and seeing the smile come to his face when Mommy walks into the room. I plan diligently for outings after work. It is no longer about my needs, but our son's. If I decide to run errands after picking him up, I plan to have enough pampers, bottles, wipes, and of course a change of clothes. I make arrangements with my sitter to watch Jeffrey every other Tuesday while I go to the salon. Do you have a plan in place to accommodate the changes that will take place? As much as I desired to be a mother, there are times that I pray for strength to handle all of the responsibilities. I remember praying and telling God I know I prayed for this and I am happy to be a mommy, but I need strength to handle being wife, mother, daughter, ministry, work, extended family, and friends. There have been times that I felt that I was pushing myself too much; which is not good for my family or me. It is once again through pray and waiting to hear what God's response is to my prayer to know that I needed to let some things go and it was okay to say no to invitations. I had to learn to find a healthy balance by not taking on any false obligations and remaining in my lane. God has given me the strength to not feel guilty when I cannot make it to every event that I am asked to attend.

TEMPTATION
(Die Daily)

No Temptation has seized you except what is common to man. And God who is faithful: he will not let you be tempted beyond what you can bear. But when you are tempted, he will also provide a way out so that you can stand up under it. ~ I Corinthians 10:13 NIV

1. What is your temptation?

Talking when you should be listening
Expecting when you should be blessing
Mumbling when you should be praising
Procrastinating when you should be doing
Telling when you should be keeping
Accepting when you should be rejecting/resting
Taking when you should be giving
Imitating when you should be original
Obnoxious when you should be quiet
Negative when you should be positive

2. It all depends on whose hands it is in?

2 Corinthians 4:7-12 NIV states, [7]But we have this treasure in jars of clay to show that this all-surpassing power is from God and not from us. [8]We are hard pressed on every side, but not crushed; perplexed, but not in despair; [9]persecuted, but not abandoned; struck down, but not destroyed. [10]We always carry around in our body the death of Jesus, so that the life of Jesus may also be revealed in our body. [11]For we who are alive are always being given over to death for Jesus' sake, so that his life may be revealed in our mortal body. [12]So then, death is at work in us, but life is at work in you.

A basketball in Tiger Woods hands is not the same as a basketball in Michael Jordan's hands. A golf club is not the same in Michael Jordan's hands as a golf club in Tiger Woods'. My husband adorning himself in a pilot's uniform does not make him a pilot. Jeff would have to make some preparations in order to make the transition from Coach King to a pilot. He would have to study and enroll in courses required by the FAA to meet their standards. With endurance, he can consistently accomplish all the obstacles that are required to become an official pilot then he can wear the title and uniform with honor. It is the same with our feelings. We can own up to what we are feeling and seek ways to heal, or we can pretend they do not exist and dig ourselves deeper into a place that is unrealistic. It is your choice to choose how you deal with pain and disappointment on your journey. Will you use the experience to gain a closer relationship with Christ and encourage others at the same time? Will you lead by example of how you trust and praise God regardless of the circumstance? Experience has taught me that Living daily for Christ requires dying daily to self.

Coffee Beans[7]

A carrot, an egg, and a cup of coffee...

You will never look at a cup of coffee the same again. A young woman went to her mother and told her about her life and how things are so hard for her. She did not know how she was going to make it and wanted to give up. She was tired of fighting and struggling. It seemed as soon as one problem was solved a new one arose.

Her mother took her to the kitchen, filled three pots with water, and placed each on a high fire. Soon the pots came to a boil. In the first, she placed carrots in the second eggs and in the last ground coffee beans. She let them sit and boil without saying a word.

In about twenty minutes, she turned off the burners. She fished the carrots out and placed them in a bowl. She

---

[7] allinspiration.com, contributed by an anonymous submitter, or its source is unknown

pulled the eggs out and placed them in a bowl. Then she ladled the coffee out and placed it in a bowl.

Turning to her daughter, she asked, "Tell me what you see?" "Carrots, eggs, and coffee," she replied. Her mother brought her closer and told her to feel the carrots. She did and noted that they were soft. The mother then asked the daughter to take an egg and break it. After pulling off the shell, she observed the hard-boiled egg. Finally, the mother asked the girl to sip the coffee. The daughter smiled, as she tasted the rich aroma. The daughter then asked what that means, mother.

Her mother then explained that each of these objects faced the same adversity.... boiling water.... each reacted differently. The carrot went in strong, hard and unrelenting. However, after being subjected to the boiling water, it softened and became weak. The egg had been fragile. Its thin outer shell had protected its liquid interior, but after sitting through the boiling water, its inside became hardened. The ground coffee beans were unique, however, after they were in the boiling water. They had changed the water, "Which are you?" She asked the daughter.

When adversity knocks at your door, how do you respond? Are you a carrot, an egg or a coffee bean? Think of this "Which am I?" Am I the carrot that seems strong, but with pain and adversity do I wilt and become soft and lose my strength? Am I the egg that starts with a malleable heart, but changes with the heat? Did I have a fluid spirit but after a death, a break up, a financial hardship or other trial, have I become hardened and stiff? Does my shell look the same but the inside and I bitter, tough with a stiff spirit, and hardened hear? Or am I like the coffee bean? The bean actually changes the hot water, the very same circumstances that bring the pain. When the water gets hot, it releases the fragrance and flavor. If you are like the bean when things are at their worst you get better and change the situation around you. When the hour is the darkest and trials their greatest, do you elevate yourself to another level? How do you handle adversity? Are you a carrot, an egg or a coffee bean? Count your blessings not your problems....

EPILOGUE

Family Friends and Well wishers

    I will never forget some of the things said to us during our season of waiting. It is best to offer a listening ear and a shoulder to lean on. I was told countless times to relax and to stop thinking about it and it will happen. Well I would like to share that I never stopped thinking about it. If you have not walked in the shoes of a person dealing with fertility you really do not understand how we feel. Several ladies have shared their feelings of frustration with some of the comments that others have made. We did not choose to travel this road or to feel the way that we do. I would like to be the spokesperson to say that the insensitive comments hurt and we try to make the best of it but deep down if we are not careful it can put a wedge between us and those who make the comments. I love my mom (mother of 6) and my sisters who have 12 children between the three of them for never making me feel bad about how I felt. My oldest sister, Sonya, even invited me into her room one family reunion and shared with me the miracle of how my niece was conceived and how when God does it it's done. I carried my sister's words with me and believed that if He did it for her that He would do it for me. I carried my sister's testimony with me. It encouraged me when I was told that I had one tube blocked and one clear and the chances of us conceiving was every other month. That testimony carried each time a procedure did not work for us. I was able to stand on God's word of not showing favoritism to anyone because in His word He did it for others therefore He would do it for me.

I thank God for Vicki telling me that God knew the exact date of conception and my child's birthday and that I was to praise Him and wait until the Lord revealed it to me. I encourage each of you to surround yourself around positive people who will support you even when you are feeling low. I thank God for Vicki who continuously prayed for me and encouraged me when I needed it. Vicki is an example for many because though she didn't experience it personally she was wise enough to just listen and she always gave a positive outlook regardless of how it looked. I remember when I called Vicki to share my news of being pregnant she cried tears of joy and right there on the phone we had our own praise and worship session honoring God for being faithful to his word.

Jeff and I now have now been married for almost 14 years. Our son is 4 years old and continues to bring joy to our lives daily. Jeff is satisfied with our son and is content with having an only child. However, for me deep down inside I still desire to have another child. My cycle was almost a month late, but a blood test I recently took came back negative. I must admit that the idea of possibly being pregnant a second time was an exciting thought for me. I began to calculate a possible due date before I remembered past disappointments and stopped myself before yet another flood of emotions began. Many have asked me why I continue to host TRUST meetings since I have conceived and now have a miracle baby, my answer is always the same, "I remember and will never forget that season of waiting." I dedicate my life to encouraging as many ladies that I can. God is able to do just what He said He would do.

It is best for you to seek God as to what His plan is for your life. My friends John and Veronica have an adorable son who was conceived through in vitro fertilization. Our friends Terence and Michele were blessed with a handsome son through adoption. Although each of us was blessed with our sons through three different methods it doesn't make us love them any less. Each one of us has our own testimony to share in order to bring God glory. Pray and seek God, wait to hear his answer, and then stand on whatever He tells you; regardless of who may try to discourage you. God is not a man that He should lie. God sees your tears. He hears your prayers. He is comforting you even when you may not feel like it. *You Are Not Alone* in your pain. I am praying for you. If I could, I would reach out and hug you or hold your hand to comfort you. Please know from this point on that someone is always praying for you. You must believe whatever He tells you regarding your promised child and remember *You Are Not Alone*.

TESTIMONIALS

On a Christian retreat, I explained to those sitting near me that my husband and I were struggling to have children, when Helen began speaking to the crowd. Within minutes it was evident that Helen had experienced many of the same things I had. God used that time to show His faithfulness to me and those sitting near me, that day. The message was clear: He does hear the cry of our hearts and timing is His specialty. Soon, I began attending T.R.U.S.T. meetings and gaining encouragement from others going through infertility issues. God has spoken mightily through Helen and the group that she gathers on a monthly basis. Her story and ministry continue to bring life to me and my husband as we follow God's direction for building our family. I am so grateful for her faithfulness in answering God's call.

Estelle

T.R.U.S.T. has been a tremendous blessing to me. I am involved in several online Christian based fertility groups, but nothing local any longer. It is wonderful to have a group of women come together who believe in the Lord and can uplift one another in prayer. Helen King continues to be a blessing to the group as its lead servant. She has not faltered in helping minister to women with fertility issues even though she has already received her own miracle child. She has never forgotten hurting and waiting women, and their plight. May God bless her and the women of T.R.U.S.T.

Mrs. V. McBride

TRUST was a major foundational part of my healing process toward the belief of motherhood in my life. I attended my first TRUST meeting 6 years ago with neutral expectation due to the disappointment of being told motherhood is not a realistic desire for me. When I opened my heart to the leadership of this ministry I began to witness God blessing my life in ways I would have never received before.

My husband and I have recently experienced the joy of bringing a two year old into our lives. He was badly beaten, bruised from head to toe, but his beauty is indescribable. I thank T. R. U. S. T. For supporting me while God prepared me to support him.

T. R. U. S. T. Helped me believe in my dreams, now I am floating on LOVE because of the word he sings, MOMMY!!

Joel Daniell McCray

TRUST has filled and built my heart with forgiveness, faith, and strength. I have a new mission since I allowed TRUST to be a part of my life.

At first, I was very hesitant about attending a TRUST meeting. I didn't think talking to a bunch of strangers about my miscarriage would help me overcome my fears of becoming pregnant again. Boy was I wrong. TRUST helped me gain self-confidence by providing me with specific scriptures desperately needed for answers to my questions. Also, hearing other testimonies and confessions of other members, kept reminding me that I wasn't alone.

When I experienced my second miscarriage, I handled my tragedy totally different. I was hurt, but not angry. I didn't question God's decision. Most of all, the incident didn't discourage me from trying again. I couldn't have done this without TRUST

This new knowledge has strengthened my faith and has given me the power to continue my dream of having a healthy baby boy.

I praise God T.RUST was created and for sending me an "Earth Angel" (You).

Delshonna Harris
My new favorite scripture is Matthews 7. (Judging others)

I want to thank God for Helen being obedient to His voice to start The T.R.U.S.T. Ministry. I ended up with two blessings: A great Spiritual Friend and a Powerful Support Group. God brought us together at a time such as this to bless each other in many ways than one. This Ministry has helped me to stand on God's Word no matter how long it takes. Always remember God's timing is not our timing. God's Word also tells us that when you have done all you can just stand. God has blessed my husband and I to adopt a fine and wonderful little boy. In the meantime, we are holding on to God's promise that I will conceive children like Sarah and Hannah in my due season. Helen, God loves you and so do I.

God bless you,

Rhonda Russell

ABOUT THE AUTHOR

Helen Jackson King is a teacher in Broward county. She is a graduate of Miami Northwestern High School. She earned her Bachelor of Science in Elementary Education from Bethune-Cookman College.

Helen is the founder of T.R.U.S.T. (Totally Relinquishing Unto our Savior Today/Tomorrow) a Christian support group that encourages couples who are facing struggles due to infertility. Since the first T.R.U.S.T. meeting on December 28, 2002, 63 babies have been born.

OUR MIRACLE CHILD
Jeffrey Paul King II